MEMBERS ONLY

A Powerful New Way to Grow Your Practice

Table of Contents

Foreword

Because much of my work involves traveling the world keynoting conferences and developing training programs for *Fortune 500* companies, I only have limited time to counsel individual clients and their families—part of my work that I truly love. Therefore, out of necessity, I have become very selective regarding the clients with whom I choose to work.

As a result of becoming selective, I noticed a fascinating outcome for my practice: Rather than seeking out another psychologist, people started coming out of the woodwork, hoping I would take them on as clients. The powerful, psychological phenomenon of covert persuasion that is engaged when someone wants to feel a part of a *selective and exclusive* group, it seemed, was magically drawing these folks to me! These people did not want to be left out of a "club" where others (whom I had already selected) were seen as having some sort of real advantage. This powerful phenomenon is the essence of *Members Only*. Its authors have written a masterpiece that can be very quickly read and put into action.

During these highly competitive and uncertain economic times, financial advisors need the psychological tools necessary to stay above their competition, maintain their client base, and attract new business. Despite achieving supreme success in selling, if they cannot convince potential clients that working with their firm is the "winning ticket," they won't retain those clients or generate a steady referral stream. The pages of this book are filled with real-life examples of a firm going the extra mile to care for their present and potential clients. The firm is like a family, with every employee imparting a carefully crafted and compelling image.

It has been proven that a first and often lasting impression is made within the first four seconds of meeting someone. The authors of this gem show you how your firm can create an experience that will rivet potential clients immediately, make them feel special, engage your services, and ultimately motivate them to refer their friends and relatives as well.

I'm confident that you will be riveted within the first four seconds of reading this book!

Jack N. Singer, Ph.D.
President and CEO, Psychologically Speaking
Licensed Clinical, Industrial/Organizational, and
Sport Psychologist
Diplomate, American Academy of Behavioral
Medicine

Introduction

WHAT MAKES SOMEONE WANT TO BELONG TO a private club? Words like platinum, preferred, crown, regal, royal, star, elite, and others—flattering word choices used to describe so many separate organizations—hint at the underlying motivation of their respective members. People want to feel special.

This fact is certainly no secret to the businesses that enhance loyalty and drive revenue through programs aimed at rewarding their customers with special privileges. Frequent flyers avoid lines when boarding airplanes. Repeat shoppers receive special discounts. Big spenders are offered platinum credit cards. Preferred guests get access to private lounges and free use of hotel health clubs. The proliferation of such benefits proves that these kinds of strategies can contribute toward profitability.

How many of such "clubs" do you belong to? I personally belong to more than I can count. There's the one at my video store, bank, two of the supermarkets where I shop, the drugstore, the shoe shine stand at the airport, the place that washes my car, and the men's store where I buy my ties. But does belonging to any of these "clubs" make me special? Not really. Basically, these are rewards programs, not exclusive clubs.

On the other hand, there are clubs that offer *genuine* exclusivity—that only admit members of a socially restricted and carefully selected group. What's more, the finest among such organizations offer members the ultimate in luxury, privacy, and prestige. Despite defying the limits of political correctness, such institutions succeed in accomplishing something truly remarkable. They create an aura so powerful that people line up to join them, even if doing so means enduring waiting periods that are years long and membership dues in the hundreds of thousands of dollars. Also noteworthy is that such clubs rarely have to market themselves. Their membership base grows strictly from referrals.

Is it possible for a business to generate the same brand of appeal that the world's private clubs do? Can a company create an identity so alluring that people line up to do business with it? What would it take to make that happen?

In the following parable, you will learn four keys to building an endless referral stream by harnessing the power of exclusivity.

"I'm telling you Jim, you and Jan *have* to come to the wine tasting with us tonight."

Jim Johnson stopped concentrating on his swing and focused on his friend. "Is that the Madsen & Associates event you were telling me about?"

"Yes. It's a fun thing my advisor does for his big clients and their friends. It's at 5:30. We'll grab dinner after."

"I don't know, Steve, the last thing I want is to listen to somebody's sales pitch. I'm sure he's got an agenda."

"No, he does this to keep us informed about what's happening in the markets. It's really laid back. He gives us a market update and we drink some good wine. I know you're cynical about—"

"I'm not cynical; I'm realistic. Everybody wants something, Steve. Companies don't just do 'nice things' without expecting something in return. It's just like the 'free' vacation voucher I got in the mail yesterday. It *can* be free *if* I pay three hundred dollars in taxes and fees, and sit through their four-hour presentation. I hate that kind of thing!"

"I understand where you're coming from, but John and his office aren't like that. For starters, they're very selective about who they work with. You'd have to qualify to work with them in the first place. And secondly, they really *do* care. In fact, John is a good friend of mine. Bottom line, Carol and I just want you to come along because it will be fun. Besides, you just retired. Heaven knows you could use some good advice."

Jim had been thinking about that a lot lately, but he just couldn't bring himself to turn over his hard-earned money to a total stranger. Admittedly, this idea of "qualifying" intrigued him. *Don't financial advisors work with everyone?* he thought.

"I've been taking care of my money for a long time, and we've done just fine," he said, making up his mind.

"All right," Steve conceded, "but come along for the free wine and good conversation. I promise you won't regret it."

"I suppose I'll come for that," Jim said as he teed off, but he had no intention of turning over one red cent.

Create an Experience

THE EXTERIOR OF THE FIRM WAS FLAWLESS. JIM couldn't help but marvel at the sidewalk. Not one speck of dirt or a single cigarette butt marred the gleaming concrete. The flowers leading up to the entrance had been planted in straight lines and were freshly mulched. A large plush mat lay at the threshold monogrammed with the company's logo and the topiaries that stood on either side of the door were perfectly manicured.

"This is beautiful," he heard his wife say to Carol. He didn't want to admit it but Jan was right. He reached for the door just as it was opened by an attractive young woman who greeted them with a dazzling smile.

"Mr. and Mrs. Smith! How are you?" the woman asked, shaking Steve's hand. Carol leaned forward and gave her a hug.

"Renee, you look beautiful as always," Carol said as she stepped into the lobby.

Jim ushered his wife through the door. For a moment he forgot the polite young woman as the beauty of the office enveloped him. Large canvas artwork in ornate frames decorated the walls. Rich, dark wood covered the desk and coffee table. The overstuffed chairs looked luxurious and inviting. Even the lighting was perfect: soft and relaxing instead of harsh and blinding.

"Are these the Johnsons you told us about?"

Jim snapped back to the present as Renee reached out her hand to shake his.

"We're so excited to have you with us. We're expecting a pretty good crowd tonight so I saved you a spot."

As Renee turned, Jim caught his wife's eye and he could tell by her expression that she was impressed. After they were seated, Renee gave them each a menu.

"On these menus you'll find the three wines we'll be trying, plus tasting notes from the sommelier. We'll be getting started in about fifteen minutes, but help yourself to some fresh fruit, cheese and crackers in the conference room. Mr. and Mrs. Johnson, would you like still or sparkling water?"

They glanced at one another. "Sparkling," Jim answered.

"And would you like a wedge of lemon or lime?"

"I'll have lemon, please," Jan said.

"And the usual for you?" Renee asked the Smiths.

As she went to get their drinks, Jim said casually, "Everyone seems very nice."

"Oh, they're wonderful, Jim!" Carol exclaimed. "They're like my kids. In fact, we get an anniversary card from them every year."

"Half the time our own kids forget," Steve laughed.

The conference room, like the rest of the office, was not a disappointment. The table in the center of the room was crafted in rich detail and on it rested three silver platters decorated with arrangements of fresh fruit and cheeses cut into fancy patterns. There were two servers in the room to assist, and Jim noticed how professional they looked. Both were wearing pressed black pants and white shirts with matching black ties. They were very friendly and helpful, and seemed to be enjoying themselves as much as the guests were. Jim recalled the five-star resort where he and Jan had spent their last anniversary and was struck by the similarity of this experience.

They filled their plates and headed back to the table. Always a keen observer, Jim kept an eye out for anything out of place or untidy but he could find nothing. The entire office was spotless.

"Oh look, there's John," Carol said, pointing to a man coming into the lobby.

Jim noticed that the man was impeccably dressed in a tailored suit over a crisp shirt. His jacket was buttoned and a pocket square was neatly tucked into the front of it. He looked important and carried himself with confidence. Jim was positive they wouldn't be getting the royal treatment from him, but much to his surprise the man came straight to their table.

"I heard you guys hit the greens today. Still working on that handicap?"

"You know it," Steve said. "It's my short game that's killing me."

"When are we getting back out there? It's been what, two months now?" the man asked.

"I'm retired! I've got all the time in the world."

The man laughed. "I'll have to have you and a friend up to play at my club. I'll give you a call next week. Carol, it's so good to see you. I heard your mom was in the hospital recently. How is she?" He gave her a big hug.

"She's doing much better, thank you." Carol beamed and kissed him on the cheek.

"Mr. and Mrs. Johnson, it is such a pleasure to have you with us tonight." As he turned to leave, he shook Jim's hand firmly and with a sincere smile, added, "I really hope you enjoy yourselves."

How did he know my name? Jim thought to himself. He watched as the man moved around the room. At every table smiles lit up the clients' faces. He appeared to be an old friend, not someone who was in charge of their investments. He was adored by all and Jim wondered how the man was ever going to get the lipstick kisses off his face.

The markets were going through a severe correction and yet everyone in this office was having a good time. Could they be losing money and still be happy? Maybe John was helping them beat the market. As much as he hated to admit it, his curiosity was piqued.

Earlier that day…

Renee woke that morning with a sense of urgency. She left her house early, wanting to get to the office before everyone else so she would have time to inspect it thoroughly. The wine tastings were always big events because a number of important clients and guests would be attending. Everything had to be perfect.

As she pulled into the parking lot, she thought about what made these events so successful. *At the root of their effectiveness was the firm's ability to create an experience. The clients and guests were always made to feel special.* And what better way to do that than to give them a five-star experience? Renee knew that if things were left to chance—despite the best of intentions—mistakes would be made. *The only way to provide a consistent and high-quality level of service was to have a procedure and a checklist covering every detail.*

She parked in the back, leaving the spaces nearest the door free for guests. As she walked around the front of the building, she looked over the flowerbeds.

She bent down and used a tissue from her purse to pick up a cigarette butt someone had dropped on the sidewalk.

After disarming the alarm, she turned the TV in the lobby to CNBC and switched out the old *Wall Street Journal* for the new one. Her morning routine had a calming effect, and she felt well prepared for the day ahead. As she sat down at her desk to check her email, the door chimed and a familiar voice called out, "Good morning!"

"Hi, Andrea, how are you?"

Andrea poked her head into the office. "I'm excited about tonight. I've got RSVPs from a lot of people. It should be a really great event."

"Excellent. Once you're finished with the office opening procedures, come see me so we can go over the checklist for tonight."

Half an hour later Andrea was back in her office. "There are a few things I noticed on the way in that I want to make sure get handled before our guests arrive. Will you please call the maintenance company and have them blow off the sidewalks, spread some new mulch, and trim the topiaries? And I noticed some fingerprints on the glass. Could you do me a favor and wipe it down, please?"

Andrea nodded as she made notes.

"How many clients are we expecting and how many guests?"

"There are thirty-eight clients and a total of nine guests."

Renee pulled out her own pad and pen. "Okay—who's bringing who?"

"Let's see," Andrea said, consulting her spreadsheet. "The Walkers are bringing the Shirtons who they met in pottery class. Carl and Maria VanHorn are bringing Dave and Stella Mililani. Carl and Dave retired from Chrysler together. Mrs. Palmer is bringing three of her friends: Victoria Weller, Betty Jones, and Terri Stevenson. They're all in The Red Hat Society. And Mr. and Mrs. Tate are bringing her sister and husband who are visiting from North Carolina."

"Excellent, and have any of the guests been to our events before?"

"Yes. The Mililanis came to our mid-year market update last July."

"Yes, I remember them. Okay, the wine has been chilled and the wait staff is confirmed?"

"Check."

"Linens pressed and cheese platters ordered from the caterers?"

"Yes."

"You're really on top of things, Andrea. You'll need to meet with John to go over the guest list so he can greet everyone by name. And one more thing—it was a little on the hot side last month, so would you drop the AC a couple of degrees before we start and add it to the checklist so we don't miss it next time?"

"Absolutely. Anything else?"

"I think that covers it." Andrea stood to leave. "Oh and Andrea, thanks for all of your hard work. You're a tremendous asset to our firm."

The rest of the day passed quickly. At 4:30 Renee said good-bye to the last appointment, and the office began to flutter with excitement as employees started last-minute preparations.

Renee grabbed her pre-event checklist and began going through every room that would be seen by visitors. She stocked the bathrooms and made sure the conference room was dust-free and the table had been polished.

As she inspected Andrea's desk, she noticed the light on the phone was blinking. It was after five, so technically she could let the machine answer, but it could be a client needing help so she picked up the receiver. "Thank you for calling Madsen & Associates. This is Renee. How may I assist you?"

"You always sound so happy, Renee. This is Steve Smith. I'm sorry for calling so late, but I was wondering if you guys had any room left for a couple of my friends?"

The office was already going to be packed, but the Smiths were platinum clients and Renee knew John would want to make them happy. "For you, Mr. Smith, we'll always make room. Who are your friends?"

After hanging up, Renee found Andrea at the door checking in guests. A crowd was developing so she grabbed a clipboard and began to help. "We've had a last minute addition," she said to Andrea. "The Smiths are bringing Jim and Jan Johnson. Do we have any space left?"

Andrea glanced at her clipboard. "Whatever it takes, I'll make room!"

"Great. You're a lifesaver. I better go brief John on the changes."

She found her boss in his office putting the finishing touches on his presentation. "Just wanted to make sure you have everything you need. So far, forty-five of the guests have arrived. We're still waiting on the last four. The Smiths called in around five. They're bringing Jim and Jan Johnson. Apparently Steve and Jim met on the golf course and play together quite a bit. In fact, they were playing today."

"Have I met the Johnsons before?"

"Not according to the records, but remember, you did play golf with Steve eight weeks ago."

"Yes, I remember."

"And I noticed that Carol's mom was in the hospital at the end of last month—just in case you want to inquire about her. It's 5:15 so I'll let you finish up."

As Renee headed to the kitchen to check on the wait staff, she saw a group of people approaching the main entrance. Before they could reach the door she rushed to open it. "Mr. and Mrs. Smith! How are you? Are these the Johnsons you told us about? We're so excited to have you with us. We're expecting a pretty good crowd tonight so I saved you a spot."

After seating the Smiths and their guests, Renee stepped into the kitchen. "Everything ready in here?"

"We're just finishing up," the server said.

"Okay everyone," John said, poking his head around the door, "I'm ready to get started."

Renee had made sure that all of the lists had been checked and rechecked so that not even the smallest detail was missed. Every employee knew what was expected of them so they could proceed with confidence. Now it was showtime. Renee took a deep breath and followed John out.

A few days later...

Jim sat at the breakfast table sipping his coffee and thinking about the impeccable service shown by the Madsen office. He glanced down at the card that had arrived in the mail thanking him and Jan for attending the wine tasting. It had been signed by the entire office. The day before that, he had received a phone call from Renee, the office manager, letting him know that they were welcome at any events in the future.

What kind of business does that? He wondered. Jan brought her coffee to the table and picked up the thank-you card.

"I know what you're thinking," she said, pushing the phone to his side of the table, "and you should do it. You've said yourself we need someone who can help us manage our investments properly. Now that you're retired we can't afford to do this alone.

And what if something happens to you? What will I do?"

Jim looked at his wife. He knew she was right, but now a new thought entered his mind. "You know I've heard that they don't work with everyone. They're really exclusive."

"Good. That's the kind of company I want to be a part of."

"They have minimum account requirements we probably can't meet."

"You'll never know unless you call to make an appointment. Besides, they did offer to meet with us free of charge to see if there is anything they can do to help. What do we have to lose?"

He picked up the phone and punched in the numbers.

It was answered on the second ring. "Good morning, thank you for calling Madsen & Associates. This is Andrea. How may I assist you?"

"Hi, Andrea, this is Jim Johnson."

"Hello, Mr. Johnson, what a pleasure to hear from you. It was so nice to meet you the other night. How are you and Mrs. Johnson doing?"

"We're good, thank you. I was actually calling to see if I could make an appointment to discuss our investments with John."

"Wonderful. I know he would love to meet with you. What day of the week is best for you?"

"Do you have anything available next Monday?"

"Yes. Would you prefer morning or afternoon?"

"We would prefer morning."

"Mr. Madsen can meet with you at 10:30."

"That sounds good."

"Excellent. So I have you down for Monday at 10:30. Now let me confirm that we have your best address on file, and if I can get your email address, I'll send you an appointment reminder."

Jim gave her the information.

"Mr. Johnson, as soon as I get off the phone I'm going to send you a packet of information. In that packet will be a list of items to bring to your first appointment as well as step-by-step directions from your home to our office. And, because we know your time is valuable, I'm going to send you an investment profile questionnaire that John asks all prospective clients to fill out and mail back to us so we can be well prepared for your appointment."

"I'm not sure I want to give out personal information like that," Jim said, feeling wary.

"I completely understand," Andrea assured him. "We ask for this information because we feel that when it comes to managing your investments, and ultimately the legacy you leave behind, we have to make sure we don't miss any critical details. It's kind of like providing a medical history to your doctor. Our confidentiality agreement included in the packet guarantees the ultimate in privacy and discretion. And don't worry; I'll even throw in a self-addressed stamped envelope for your convenience."

Jim laughed. "Okay, I'll get that right over to you."

"Thank you so much, Mr. Johnson. Is there anything else I may assist you with today?"

"No, that's it."

"Well, it's been my pleasure serving you! We'll look forward to seeing you on Monday. Have a wonderful day."

Jim hung up, impressed by the organization and efficiency of the office. There had been a lot of clients and guests at the wine tasting, yet Andrea remembered him. He felt important, and a little nervous that they might not want to work with him.

Offer Genuine Exclusivity

On monday, jim and jan arrived a few minutes early for their appointment. As he swung around the lot looking for a parking space, Jim asked Jan if she was sure she had brought all the documents John asked for.

"Yes, dear," she said, giving him a sideways glance. "Are you okay? You seem a little edgy."

He didn't want to admit to the butterflies flitting around in his stomach, so he shrugged and answered, "I just want to find a parking space and get inside on time."

Even as he spoke, Jim noticed a spot right by the door with a sign over it: Reserved. *Probably reserved for John*, he thought as he started to pass by. Jan stopped him. "Would you look at that?" she asked, pointing at the sign.

He couldn't believe it, but it actually said: RESERVED FOR MR. AND MRS. J. Johnson. "Do you think that's us?" Jan asked incredulously.

He smiled and swung into the spot. "Do you know any other Mr. and Mrs. J. Johnsons?"

"This just keeps getting better and better," Jan said as Jim opened her door and helped her out.

The lobby was just as beautiful as Jim remembered. The receptionist smiled as she came around the desk to shake their hands. "Mr. and Mrs. Johnson, welcome back. I'm Andrea. Have a seat and I'll let John know you're here. In the meantime here's a refreshment menu to look over. I'll be back to serve you in just a few minutes."

Jim sat down next to Jan and looked at the menu. "Look at all the stuff they offer," Jan said pointing at the list of teas. "There must be ten choices here. Not to mention soft drinks and coffees."

Jim perused the list of fresh baked cookies and was amazed that they even had a sugar-free option. Jan had been diagnosed with diabetes five years before, and to support her he had pretty much given up sweets. Now he could enjoy a chocolate chip cookie and not feel guilty.

Andrea returned and took their order. They still had a few minutes until their appointment time so Jim settled back into the comfortable leather chair and picked up a golf magazine. Jan chose a book about exotic travel destinations. As they were reading, John's office door opened and he stepped out with an attractive couple in their mid-fifties. Jim was sure he had seen them at the wine tasting.

"Thanks again, John," the woman said, giving him a hug and a kiss on the cheek.

"Any time, Mary."

"I won't kiss you but I will shake your hand," Mary's husband said laughing.

"I'll take it," John said, giving the man a warm handshake.

After he had shown them out, he turned to Jim. "Good morning, Mr. and Mrs. Johnson. It's such a pleasure to see you again! I'll be with you in a few moments. Please make yourselves at home while you wait."

He returned to his office just as Andrea brought their drinks and cookies served on real china. She handed each of them a black cocktail napkin with the company's logo embossed in gold.

As Jim ate his cookie, he marveled that even the smallest detail had been cared for. The television in the lobby was turned to CNBC, but the sound was muted so he could hear the classical music coming from invisible speakers overhead. The chair was comfortable, the magazines were current, and the air was filled with the scent of fresh baked goodies and coffee.

If we don't get in, he thought, *Jan will be so disappointed.* Admittedly, he would be too.

"Mr. and Mrs. Johnson, may I escort you to the conference room?" Andrea asked with a smile as she motioned for them to follow her.

On the conference room table, instead of platters of fruit and cheese, sat a laptop. The large flat screen television behind it read: WELCOME MR. AND MRS. Johnson. John pulled out Jan's chair and then sat across from them.

"I see you haven't lived here very long. How do you like the community?" John asked, opening their file.

"We really like it," Jim said, glancing at Jan who nodded, "Everyone's been very friendly, and the weather's great."

"I like that it's close to everything," Jan said.

"My wife feels the same way. I know you like to play golf, Jim; have you played over at Trump's new course yet?"

"No, but I hear it's amazing. I'd like to get over there eventually."

"It really is the nicest course in the area. I'd be happy to set you up a tee time."

"Thank you, I appreciate that."

"To get us started," John said, "I'd like to outline my goals for this meeting. I'm sure you also have some goals, and I want you to feel free to bring them up. I want to make sure we address everything that's important to you."

Jim nodded. So far he liked what he was hearing.

"Our primary goal during this meeting is to get to know each other. Here at Madsen & Associates, we have a thriving practice. Obviously this doesn't allow us to work with everyone, so we are very selective about the people we choose to work with. It has never been our goal to be all things to all people, but rather, to be all things to a few people. It is only by carefully selecting our clients that we are able to provide the level of personalized service that we do. For this reason, before we take on any new clients, we are careful to gather enough information to ensure they pass four key tests. We will be looking at all four of these tests together today.

"Our first test is the *Chemistry Test*. I'm proud to say I like all of my clients, and I'm committed to making sure that never changes." John smiled. "During today's meeting we are going to see whether we feel like we have the chemistry to work together for the long run.

"Our second test is the *Goal Test*. I'm going to ask you a lot of questions about your goals today. My objective is to see if they are achievable. If I don't feel they are achievable, I would rather not help you fail."

"That sounds reasonable," Jan murmured.

"I'm glad. Third is our *Worth Test*. As I mentioned, I don't work with everyone. In fact, I specialize in working with high net-worth clients."

Jim's heartbeat sped up. He wondered if he would pass this test.

"Lastly, and most important is the *Value Test*. If we can't add value to what you're currently doing, there's no reason to make a change.

"At this point, I want to open this discussion up to you. What's important to you? What are your goals?"

Jim was prepared for this question and began outlining everything he hoped to gain if indeed they were accepted as clients.

An hour and a half later, John walked them out to the lobby. "It has been a tremendous pleasure meeting with you both," he said, shaking their hands. "I'm happy we've had this opportunity to get to know each other. Sometime during the next two days, I will sit down with my team and review the notes from our meeting to ensure we are a good fit for one another. Of course, it's clear we've already passed the Chemistry Test." He smiled warmly. "Now all we need to do is analyze your goals, worth, and ultimately, what value we can bring to you. I'll have Renee contact you within the next forty-eight hours to let you know what we decide. Again, it was a pleasure getting to know you both better."

Back in the car, neither of them spoke. Finally Jan said, "What now?"

"Now," Jim said, starting the engine, "we wait."

Back inside the Madsen office, John was contemplating how the meeting went. *My best clients are*

always referrals from existing clients, John thought as he sat in his office reviewing the Johnsons' file. He was still extremely pleased with his decision to shift focus away from public marketing efforts and onto established client relationships. This client-centric business model didn't come easy to him. It had been nerve-wracking to slow down the advertising and start relying on referrals, but well worth it in the long run.

He dialed into his dictation service, and began recording the notes he had taken during his meeting with Jim and Jan. They were great people. The type of clients he would enjoy working with if they qualified.

John finished his dictation and headed to Renee's office. She looked up from her computer and smiled. "How are your meetings going?"

"Good," he said, putting a stack of files on her desk. "I just had a great meeting with the Johnsons. You should be receiving the notes I dictated in your email shortly. And just to confirm, did someone send a gift basket to the Smiths thanking them for the referral?"

"As always."

"Excellent. I'll fill you in on the details when we meet this afternoon to review the day's appointments."

After saying good-bye to his last appointment, John felt deeply satisfied. Not everyone he had met with today would qualify to work with his firm, but he felt confident he could help some of them.

A few years earlier, John had discovered an indispensable key to running a successful practice: *Exclusivity. Clients—especially the high net-worth—want to be treated special. If you work with everyone, no one feels special.* There's a reason why people prefer to shop at upscale boutiques rather than giant super-centers. At the boutique they are singled out, waited on, gushed over. Not everyone can afford to shop there, and this makes their shoppers special. Though being exclusive presented its challenges, John knew it was necessary: *If you work with everyone, you have to beg for business. If you're truly exclusive, people will beg to work with you.*

He entered the conference room and greeted his team. Taking a seat at the head of the table, he opened the first file: Jack and Lisa Carlisle.

"Well, I know I don't have to tell you what great people the Carlisles are," he said glancing up. Around the table, heads nodded in agreement. "Unfortunately, they don't meet our minimum net-worth requirements. I'd love to take their case just to help them out, but because of the time involved, it would be cost prohibitive to have a client that small. Renee, will you please send them a thank-you card and contact them personally to let them know it was a privilege meeting with them? You can also tell them that we feel the Seabert firm would be a better fit, and offer to send their contact information over."

Picking up the next file, he continued, "On to Ms. Bedford. This case isn't quite as black and white. She's $150,000 shy of meeting our minimum net worth requirement, which is not really that far off. At the same time, she's a huge center of influence in the community. That fact alone makes her a desirable client.

"The other challenge is that her income goals are unrealistic. In order to meet them, her withdrawal rate would have to be nearly 8%. And with her risk tolerance and time horizon where they are, I don't think we can sustain that."

Brian, his junior advisor, added, "One thing I know is that as far as our Value Test is concerned, we can definitely add value to what she's currently doing. In fact, if she doesn't implement some prudent strategies soon, and start following a real budget, she's going to run out of money before she runs out of life. At the very least, I think she needs some straightforward advice."

"What about our Chemistry Test?" John asked. "I know I enjoyed her company. How did she treat the staff, Renee?"

"I talked to her for a few minutes in the lobby. She seemed pleasant, and she and Andrea really hit it off. I say we take her on."

"I agree. Does everyone else?" John asked, looking around the table. It was unanimous.

"Okay, let's look at Jim and Jan Johnson's file."

Hire the Right People and Hold Them to a Written Standard

THOUGH THE DECISION ABOUT JIM AND JAN JOHNSON had been made, Renee spent the entire next day screening and interviewing applicants. She glanced down at the six-inch stack of paper on her desk and sighed. So far, 190 people had applied for the administrative assistant position they needed to fill. It had been a daunting task to screen so many applicants. At times she thought about calling a staffing agency to do the job, but she knew that finding the right people was something they could not trust a stranger to do.

Since the beginning, she and John had worked closely together to find the right employees. From an outsider's perspective everything the firm did seemed effortless, but in reality, it only ran smoothly because the right people were in place.

The screening process was rigorous. The candidates submitted to a telephone interview, multiple face-to-face interviews, a personality profile, drug test, and background screening. Renee realized that some would think their methods were extreme, but it was better to spend the time and energy to find just one quality employee than to waste any time on the wrong ones.

She had whittled the stack of 190 down to ten qualified candidates. Four of them were coming in for interviews that day. Renee thought carefully about the questions she would ask during this second face-to-face interview. At this point, she knew each of these candidates possessed the necessary skills for the position; now it was time to see if they had the personality to match.

Her first question, *tell me about a time when you helped someone*, would let her know if the applicant was a Good-Samaritan-type person. In order for a company like Madsen & Associates to prosper, they had to hire people who derived pleasure from helping others, those who viewed helping their fellow man as a moral obligation.

What is your preferred method of communication was a question she always asked because she felt that people who liked to communicate face-to-face or by telephone instead of by instant message or text were generally more social and outgoing, something they looked for.

When she asked *what inspires and motivates you in a job,* this would tell her much about the person's work-related priorities. If their priorities aligned with the company's priorities, the relationship would likely succeed.

You can teach people skills, but you can't teach them personality, Renee thought. *If they aren't friendly and service-oriented by nature, telling them they need to be will accomplish little.* Satisfied that her questions would enable her to decide if any of the applicants would be given further consideration, she checked her watch and went to the lobby to meet the first person.

Renee remembered the woman from her initial interview. As she reached out to shake her hand, she was glad to see she looked just as professional as last time, classic navy-blue suit, pumps, just the right amount of makeup, and a few well-chosen pieces of jewelry.

"It's nice to see you again, Julie. Let's head back to the conference room."

Once they were seated, Renee began.

"I realize this is the second time we've had you back which means we're very interested in getting to know you better."

Julie smiled, "I'm excited about this prospect. Everything I've learned about Madsen & Associates convinces me this would be a good long-term fit. This is the company I want to work for."

"Excellent," Renee said. "We're happy to hear that. I have a few more questions I would like to ask you."

Renee listened intently to Julie's answers and was pleased with what she heard. Julie was everything the firm was looking for in an employee. When the interview was over, Renee slid a crisp piece of paper across the table.

"I have something very important I would like to share with you. What you are looking at is a copy of what we call the "Madsen & Associates Service Credo." In short, these are the principles that all of us at Madsen & Associates live by. This forms the foundation of our client service, and every employee is expected to know these by heart. More than that, everyone—myself included—is expected to meet or exceed these standards at all times. Failing to live up to these standards is not an option. This is one of the things that make us different—that makes us excellent. Please take a minute to read these over, and then I'd like to know what you think."

Madsen & Associates Service Credo

- Use a warm, friendly, and sincere greeting at every interaction. Always smile. When others are speaking, give them your undivided attention. Strive to anticipate their needs and satisfy them whenever possible.

- There is nothing more important than assisting a client. If a client has a need or concern, you must help them without delay. If you do not have the authority or ability to fill their need, you must notify management immediately.

- Any defects in the property or procedures of Madsen & Associates should be corrected or reported to management immediately. All work areas must be kept neat, clean, and organized at all times.

- Your personal appearance is a reflection of you and our company. Strictly adhere to the

conservative, professional clothing standards outlined in our policy manual.

When she was finished Renee said, "Do you
think you are the type of person who could live up
to these standards? Tell me why."

Julie thought a moment then replied, "I am definitely the type who can live up to these standards.
In fact, I try to live up to these standards every day
in my personal life. I believe that if you care about
people, view others as important, and care about
the company you work for, these things will come
naturally."

Renee felt extremely pleased as she shook Julie's
hand and thanked her. She promised she would be
in touch to schedule a final interview with John. As
she headed back to her office she knew that Julie
would be a perfect addition.

A few minutes later, John poked his head into
her office. "How are the interviews coming?"

"I think we found her," Renee said as she told
him about Julie.

"That's great news. I know everyone has had to
pick up extra slack since we let Susan go, but it just
goes to show that there are always quality people

available. I hated having to terminate her, but when you're committed to providing world-class service, you need world-class employees. That's why you and I always sit down and evaluate everyone each quarter. If someone isn't performing at an A-plus level, it's our job to get them there or replace them."

"You're absolutely right," Renee said.

"It'll make us stronger in the long run. By the way, have you called the Johnsons?"

Renee smiled. "I'm picking up the phone right now."

Jan Johnson pushed her shopping cart up and down the organic food aisle. Other shoppers bustled around her, but she paid no attention. Her thoughts were centered on one thing: a call from the Madsen office. Yesterday she had fretted they would call with bad news, but with forty-eight hours drawing to a close, she now fretted they wouldn't call at all.

She thought about the conversation she had with Carol earlier that morning. Carol, who received an invitation to John Madsen's annual Dancing Under the Stars event for charity, gushed that it was *the* social event of the year. And it's for such a good cause, Jan thought as she made her way up the aisle for the fifth time. She hadn't wanted Carol to know how disappointed she was that she didn't receive an invitation, so she feigned excitement when Carol said she was going dress shopping.

Deep down, Jan was green with envy. Not just over the client events she might miss out on, but because John and his office were special. Everyone was so kind and John was so knowledgeable. She would feel secure knowing he was keeping watch over their retirement.

"Why am I getting so worked up about this?" she wondered aloud. A woman glanced in her direction and Jan turned away, embarrassed. *If we don't get in, there are other advisors we can work with,* she thought. But she knew she would never be as happy or at ease with someone else.

Jim came around the corner carrying a loaf of bread. "Are you still looking for rolled oats?" he asked.

It suddenly dawned on Jan how long she had been pushing her cart up and down the aisle. *No wonder people were looking at me strangely,* she thought.

She grabbed the oats and dropped them in the cart. "I'm ready," she said, heading for the checkout.

She didn't want to mention her feelings to Jim. She knew he was as anxious as she was. As they were loading groceries into the trunk of their car, the cell phone in Jim's pocket rang. They stared at each other a moment and Jan could see the tension in Jim's face as he answered.

"Hello? Hi, Renee."

Jan's heart fluttered.

"Uh huh…uh huh. Okay. Yes, that will be fine. Thank you, Renee. Yes, us too."

He disconnected and put the phone back in his pocket. "Well?" Jan asked, trying to read his expression.

He was quiet a moment then said, "We're in!"

Jan hadn't realized she was holding her breath until it burst from her lungs. She threw her arms around Jim and hugged him tightly. "You know what this means, right?" she said grinning.

"What?"

"I need a new dress."

Focus on Referrals

THREE MONTHS LATER, JOHN SAT ACROSS FROM the Johnsons. "It's hard to believe we've already been working together this long," he said smiling. "How would you say your experience has been with our firm so far?"

"It's been wonderful," Jim exclaimed. "You've exceeded all of our expectations, and your staff is incredible. I have to say it's been so nice not having to check the markets every day because I know our accounts are in good hands."

"Thank you for all of your help, John," Jan said.

"It's my pleasure."

As he helped Jim and Jan set up a college fund for their newest granddaughter, he knew those words were true. His clients were more than just business associates; they were friends. This is precisely why it was so hard for him to ask for referrals. Over the years though, experience had taught him how critical it was to ask for referrals. Time and again, his mind would go back to a statistic he heard at a conference some years before: "20% of clients will give you referrals no matter what; 20% of clients will never give you referrals, even if you ask. But 60% of clients will only give referrals if you ask." This was the 60% he was after.

Referrals were the primary way he grew his business, but he knew that if he asked for them the wrong way it would make him seem desperate. With a thriving and exclusive practice, desperate was the last thing John wanted to seem. The old days of handing his clients a phonebook and asking them for the numbers of ten people they knew were long gone.

The key to successfully asking for referrals was this: *Don't ask the client to do you a favor by giving referrals. Let the client know you're willing to do them a favor by accepting the people they refer.* This small change in approach made all the difference.

"Mr. and Mrs. Johnson, before our meeting ends, there is something very important I want to talk to you about. The two of you are exactly the type of clients I love working with. In fact, if I could put folks like you and the Smiths in a machine and clone you, I would."

Jim and Jan laughed.

"Not only are you an absolute delight to be around," John continued, "but as you already know, you meet all of our firm's criteria. You may recall when we first met I told you it was never my goal to be all things to everyone, but rather, all things to a few. For that reason, I keep my practice fairly small, which means I can't work with everyone.

"However, from time to time, openings do come up. And in my experience, the best way to fill those openings is with the friends and family of my best clients—clients just like you. So here's the offer I would like to extend: In my schedule each week, I leave one or two appointments open for referrals from my top clients. So if you ever know of anyone who you think could use my help, just give me a call and we can discuss it. Now I'm not a miracle worker, but I'll always do my very best to help them."

"Thank you, John, that's wonderful," Jan said, beaming.

"Now, sometimes, people don't feel comfortable making an appointment with an advisor they've never met, so if it's easier, you can bring them to any one of my events. And let me assure you, you don't have to worry whether they will meet my criteria. I would never expect you to prequalify someone. Just know that if you give me their name, we're going to roll out the red carpet for them."

"Thank you again, John. We know how busy you are," Jim said, smiling.

At the door, Jan gave him a kiss on the cheek and Jim gripped his hand in a hearty shake. "I'm looking forward to another round of golf in the near future," he said as they headed out of the office.

Still smiling, John turned to greet his next appointment. "Mr. and Mrs. Stevens, it's so nice to see you again. I'll be with you in just a moment. Please make yourselves comfortable and enjoy some refreshments."

Another referral. As John prepared for his meeting with the Stevens' he hoped they would be as wonderful as Jim and Jan.

Weeks after Jim and Jan had moved their retirement savings to Madsen & Associates, Jim was enjoying a round of golf with an old friend. He watched as Ray's ball dropped onto the green five feet from the cup.

"Nice shot," he said as he chose his next club.

"I'd be happy to give you some pointers," Ray joked.

"I'm sure you would. Speaking of pointers, have you thought anymore about coming with me to John's economic forecast meeting this week?"

"I don't know, Jim. I've heard he's a good advisor, but I've also heard he doesn't work with everyone. He probably wouldn't work with me."

"It's a good thing that they're exclusive," Jim said. "It means you'll get better service." He slapped his friend on the shoulder.

"Listen, John is a good friend of mine. Jan and I have been to dinner at his house on numerous occasions. Just this week he sent her a copy of this book on exotic destinations that she noticed in his office and fell in love with. I'm probably going to have to take her to Fiji now for our next anniversary. Bottom line is, John's a great guy. He's completely trustworthy and if I ask him, he'll meet with you."

"Let me think about it."

"Okay, but come to the workshop anyway. I promise you won't regret it."

Afterword

THE STORY YOU JUST READ MAY BE FICTIONAL, but the concepts on which it is based are not. The *Members Only* method of growing your business works. It has worked for the authors of this book, it has worked for hundreds of their followers, and it can work for you!

The four keys we outlined on the preceding pages require effort to put in place, but once they are operational, people will line up to seek your professional advice. Simple human psychology dictates that this approach will be effective. People want to feel special and they want to do business with professional organizations—precisely what *Members Only* is all about.

While the concepts in this book are presented in simple parable style, we must realistically acknowledge that the systems behind them require significant time, energy, and patience to develop. This, frankly, is why most advisors do not use this approach. It requires too much work for them.

Another reason why many advisors will not use the *Members Only* approach is because the idea of turning business away makes them almost physically ill. Some don't see the value of making a short-term sacrifice in exchange for a long-term gain. Others see the value, but they just can't muster the courage to change. They choose instead to accept every client and deal with their burgeoning service load later.

What about you? Do you think the *Members Only* model can work for your practice? If so, it is likely that a fundamental shift in the way you operate will be required. Whether or not to make this shift is a decision to be weighed carefully. If you present yourself as exclusive but don't maintain *genuine* exclusivity, people will see your efforts as a mere sales ploy. Harnessed properly though, the power of exclusivity can work for you! It can free up your time, lower your stress level, and grow your book of business!

If you decide that the *Members Only* way is for you, let us know. We will be more than happy to help you bring it to life.

Your partners in success,
Robert Sofia
Thomas Fross
Robert Fross

The Authors

Robert Sofia is a nationally recognized author, award-winning public speaker, and practice management thought leader. He has developed marketing strategies for *Fortune 500* companies, personally coaches hundreds of financial advisors nationwide, and is the COO and cofounder of Platinum Advisor Marketing Strategies. Robert holds his General Securities and Investment Advisor registrations from the Financial Industry Regulatory Authority (FINRA), and has helped build two multimillion-dollar producing financial firms—one as the vice president of marketing, and the other as company vice president.

Robert writes for a number of industry journals and mainstream publications including *The Huffington Post, AdvisorOne, Investment Advisor, Senior Market Advisor, National Underwriter, ProducersWEB,* and various broker dealer publications. He is author of *The Complete Idiot's Guide to Business Success In Your 20's and 30's,* an honorary Apex Society member, and a *Power 30 Under 30* award recipient.

Thomas Fross and **Robert Fross** have over twenty years combined experience in the financial services industry and have pioneered many of its leading practice management strategies. Their firm, Fross & Fross Financial, has distinguished itself as one of the most successful in the nation by consistently acquiring over $40 million in new assets year after year.

Robert and Thomas' success can be attributed to the development and perfection of Seven Traits necessary to attract and maintain the most sought-after clients. As accomplished public speakers, they regularly keynote broker dealer conferences, and have spoken for companies including AXA Equitable, Transamerica Capital Management, CNL, Grubb & Ellis, American Realty Capital, and others.

Early in 2009, Thomas and Robert cofounded Platinum Advisor Marketing Strategies—a turnkey marketing solution that equips financial advisors to attract and retain high net-worth clients. Through their speaking, and through Platinum, Thomas and Robert have helped thousands of financial advisors build stronger businesses.

Cate Rollins is a fiction writer who lives in Florida with her husband (a financial advisor) and two dogs. She helped bring the concepts in this book to life.

Dr. Jack Singer holds a doctorate in Industrial/Organizational Psychology and a post-doctorate in Clinical and Sport Psychology. He has taught in the Psychology Departments of seven universities, including the U.S. Air Force Academy.

Jack is the author of *The Teacher's Ultimate Stress Mastery Guide* and *Dynamic Health*, as well as several self-help programs for elite athletes and other programs for those wishing to turbocharge their self-esteem. A sought-after author and media guest, Jack appears frequently on MSNBC, CNN, FOX, ESPN, and radio talk shows throughout the United States and Canada and he has been a repeat guest on the *Glenn Beck* show.

Much of Dr. Jack's current work involves training financial advisors and sales professionals to develop the psychological secrets for ultimate success.

You can contact Dr. Jack by calling him at 800-497-9880 or emailing him at drjack@funspeaker.com. You can also visit his websites at www.funspeaker.com, www.askdrjack.com, and www.drjacksinger.com.

Services

Through Platinum Advisor Marketing Strategies, the concepts and tools outlined in this book are available in complete detail, along with everything needed to make them a reality in your own practice.

Robert Sofia, Thomas Fross, and Robert Fross are also accessible for keynotes on many topics, some of which cover the strategies outlined in this book.

Visit www.platinumadvisormarketing.com
or call 877–421–5593